Aquarius

THIS BOOK BELONGS TO:

_____

Dedicated to my son, Rye!

All rights reserved.
No part of this book may be reproduced in any form or by any means, electronic or mechanical, and no photocopying or recording, unless you have written permission from the author.

ISBN 978-1-958985-60-1

Text copyright © 2025 by Mimi Jones

www.joeysavestheday.com

A Mimi Book

# WELCOME TO: THE WONDERFUL WORLD OF ZODIACS

## AQUARIUS

Mimi Jones

Dates: Aquarius spans from January 20 to February 18.

**Element:**
Aquarius is an Air sign.

AQUARIUS

 # Ruling Planet:

Uranus and Saturn rule Aquarius

# Symbol:

The Water Bearer represents Aquarius.

Aquarius

KEEP MOVING FORWARD

## Personality:

Aquarians are known for being independent and progressive.

PROGRESS is PROGRESS

## Strength:

They are very intellectual and humanitarian.

## Color:

Their lucky colors are electric blue and silver.

*Aquarius*

## Lucky Numbers:

4, 7, 11, and 22 are lucky for Aquarius.

## Compatibility:

Aquarius gets along well with Gemini, Libra, Aries, and Sagittarius.

# LIMITED

## Dislikes:
They dislike conformity and limitations.

Aquarius

## Career:

They excel in careers that require creativity and forward-thinking.

KEEP MOVING FORWARD

# Negative Trait:

Sometimes, they can be too aloof or rebellious.

**Favorite Day:**

Saturday is their favorite day.

## SATURDAY

♥

AQUARIUS

# Hobbies:

They enjoy exploring technology, social activism, and stargazing.

# Famous Aquarians:

Some famous Aquarians include Oprah Winfrey, Harry Styles, and Thomas Edison.

## Challenges:

Aquarians need to learn to balance their ideals with emotional connections.

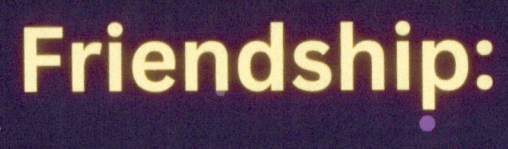

# Friendship:

They are quirky and supportive friends who bring fresh perspectives.

*friends*

# Influence:

**They inspire others with their originality and vision for the future.**

# Favorite Activities:

**Aquarians love activities that involve creativity and connecting with like-minded people.**

## Symbolic Animal:

The Water Bearer symbolizes their giving nature and flow of ideas.

## Birthstones:

### Garnet and amethyst.

If this Zodiac gem tickled your celestial fancy, then you're in for a treat! Dive into my other Zodiac delights right here:

www.mimibooks.com

**THE END!**